Horse chestnut

This tree's large, bright green leaves have five to seven oval parts, called leaflets, connected to the stem.

...rn sumac

These ...reen leaves ... have an odd number of leaflets. In the fall, the leaves turn red and gold.

Scottish pine

The leaves of this evergreen are needles, and they are protected by a thick, waxy coating.

Large leaves

Some plants have very large leaves. The giant waterlily, which grows in the Amazon, has huge, round leaves that float on water. They can grow to 8 ft (2.5 m) across!

Amazonian giant waterlily

Monkey puzzle

The leaves are long, leathery, and triangular. They are arranged in a spiral along the branches.

Thuja

This evergreen tree produces flat shoots made up of tiny, scaly leaves.

Things to find out:

....

....

....

....

....

....

....

....

....

....

....

....

....

....

....

....

....

....

....

DKfindout!

Forest

Author: Cat Hickey

Editor Katy Lennon
Designer Rhea Gaughan
US Editor Jenny Siklos
US Senior editor Shannon Beatty
Assistant editor Kritika Gupta
Art editor Rashika Kachroo
Senior editor Garima Sharma
Project art editor Nidhi Mehra
Jacket coordinator Francesca Young
Jacket designer Amy Keast
DTP designer Syed Md. Farhan
Senior picture researcher Sumedha Chopra
Pre-production producer Nikoleta Parasaki
Producer Isabell Schart
Deputy managing editor Vineetha Mokkil
Managing editors Laura Gilbert, Monica Saigal
Managing art editors Diane Peyton Jones,
Neha Ahuja Chowdhry
Art director Martin Wilson
Publisher Sarah Larter
Publishing director Sophie Mitchell

First American edition, 2017
Published in the United States by
DK Publishing, 345 Hudson Street, New York, NY 10014

Copyright © 2017 Dorling Kindersley Limited
A Division of Penguin Random House LLC
17 18 19 20 21 10 9 8 7 6 5 4 3 2 1
001–298982–July/2017

A catalog record for this book is available from the
Library of Congress.
ISBN: 978-1-4654-6232-9

DK books are available at special discounts when purchased in bulk for sales
promotions, premiums, fund-raising, or educational use. For details, contact: DK
Publishing Special Markets, 345 Hudson Street, New York, New York 10014
or SpecialSales@dk.com

Printed and bound in China

A WORLD OF IDEAS:
SEE ALL THERE IS TO KNOW
www.dk.com

Contents

Oak tree

Cacao pod

Eurasian hedgehog

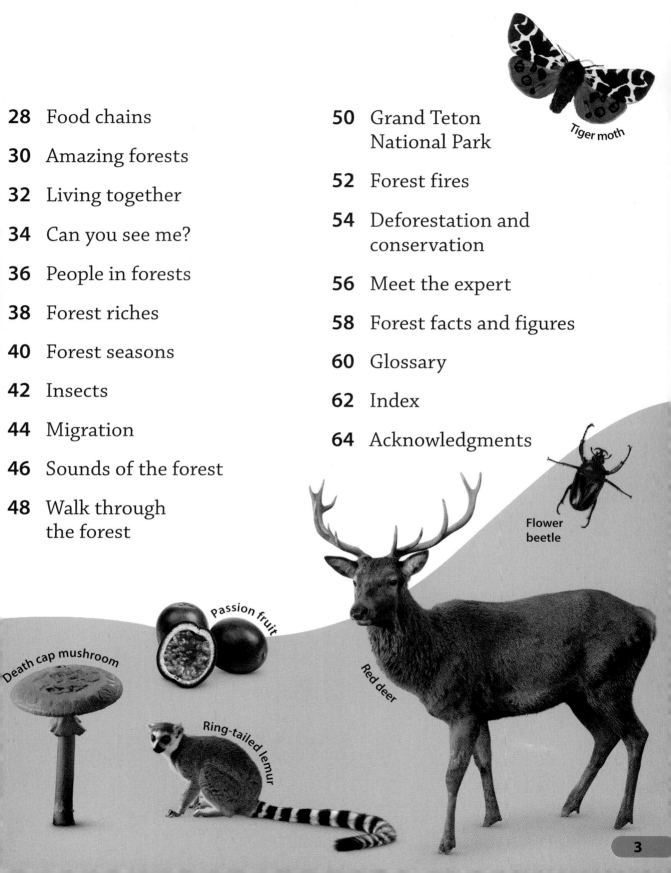

Tiger moth

Flower beetle

Death cap mushroom

Passion fruit

Ring-tailed lemur

Red deer

What is a forest?

A forest is an area of land covered by trees and other plants and flowers. Forests grow in different places all over the world and each one has lots of different types of wildlife living within it. Forests help our planet in many different ways.

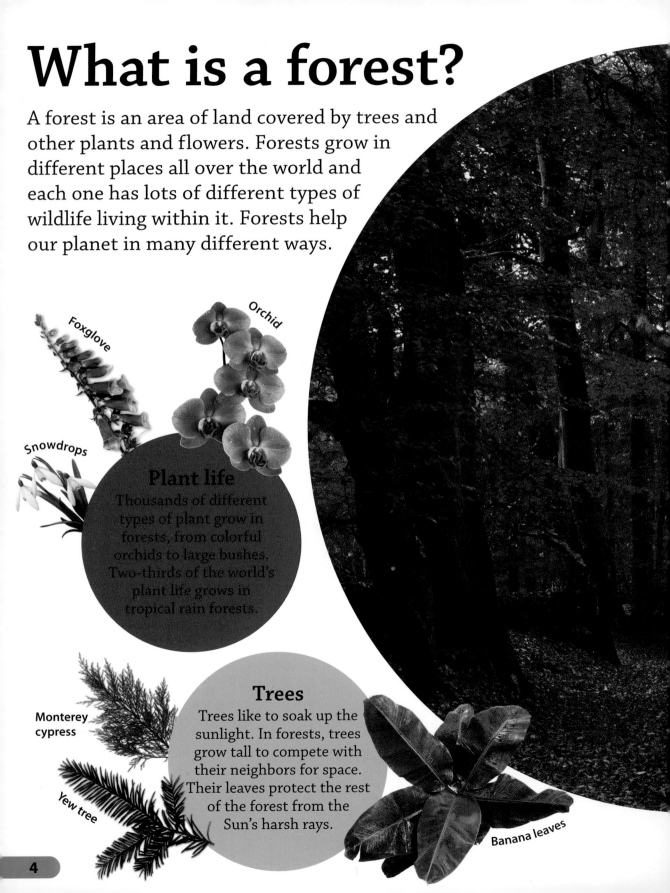

Foxglove

Orchid

Snowdrops

Plant life
Thousands of different types of plant grow in forests, from colorful orchids to large bushes. Two-thirds of the world's plant life grows in tropical rain forests.

Monterey cypress

Trees
Trees like to soak up the sunlight. In forests, trees grow tall to compete with their neighbors for space. Their leaves protect the rest of the forest from the Sun's harsh rays.

Yew tree

Banana leaves

Praying mantis

Bird's nest

Habitats

All animals need water, food, and shelter. A place that provides these things is called a habitat. Forests provide habitats for more animals than any other place on land.

Climate

The average temperature and weather conditions in an area are known as the climate. Forests can help to keep the climate steady and can even create rain!

Oxygen

Trees release the gas oxygen, which most living things need to survive. This gas is released when plants make food from sunlight, water, and the gas carbon dioxide.

Animals

Forests are home to nearly half the world's species of animals, from tiny insects to big elephants. In forests, there is rain to drink, fruit to eat, and places to shelter from predators.

Gray squirrel

British woodland in the fall

Iguana

Emergent layer from the Amazon rain forest

Forest layers

Canopy layer from a cloud forest in Costa Rica

Emergent layer

The tops of the tallest trees in the forest make up the emergent layer. These trees rise high into the sky and stretch out their leaves to soak up the sunshine.

Canopy

The canopy is the thickest layer of the forest. The trees here block out the sunlight and stop it from reaching the lower forest layers.

The understory has shorter trees that provide shelter to animals.

Forest floor from a rain forest in Costa Rica

Understory layer from a forest in Malaysia

Understory

Fewer plants grow in this layer because the sunlight cannot break through the leaves above. Twisting vines and damp mosses can be found wrapped around the tree trunks here.

REALLY?

Insects are the only creatures that can **be found in every forest layer.**

Large-leafed plants and young trees grow on the forest floor.

Forest floor

This layer is very dark and does not get much rain. It is usually home to short shrubs and fallen leaves.

Forest floor

In the rain forest, not much light reaches the forest floor. Animals that live there can use the dark to sneak up on their prey without being seen. In temperate forests, more light makes it through the canopy. Animals and plants can enjoy soaking up the Sun on the forest floor.

WHAT'S WHAT

A Elephant Forest elephants make paths by pulling down trees.

B Leopard This big cat drags its prey up trees to eat it undisturbed.

C Giant African millipede This creature's body armor and bad smell keep predators away.

D Madagascan hissing cockroach Males have horns and use them to ram other males.

E Army ants These insects are nearly blind, but detect prey by sensing movement.

F Buttress roots These wide roots anchor the tree to the forest floor.

Rain forest

Below the dense canopy, the dark forest floor is littered with fallen fruit and leaves. As they rot, their nutrients are returned to the soil.

Temperate forest

More light reaches the floor in a temperate forest than in a rain forest. Lots of animals make their homes here.

A **White-tailed deer** Plant buds and nuts are this deer's favorite foods.

B **Crab spider** This spider changes its color to blend in with the forest, so it can catch prey.

C **Vole** Burrowing under trees, voles eat dead animals such as mice.

D **Slug** The slime made by slugs helps them move and climb trees.

E **Earthworm** Plants grow better in soil that is mixed by burrowing worms.

F **Toad** This is the perfect predator for the forest floor, where lots of tasty insects live.

G **Fungi** These life forms like to grow in damp and dark conditions.

Living in the canopy

Soaking up the sunlight, this thick, leafy layer of the rain forest is full of life. Trees and plants stretch upward and animals live among the branches. Canopy life can be tricky, but everything living here has found a clever way of surviving up high. Here are some of them.

Lianas

Lianas are vines on a mission to reach the sunlight. As these plants grow, they wrap around the trunks of trees for support as they climb higher.

Just hanging!

Sloth

What's the rush? Sloths spend years slowly moving around from branch to branch, picking leaves to eat. Some just stay on a favorite tree for days on end, hanging on with their long claws.

Shlurp!

Flying fox

Although called a fox, this animal is actually a bat. It glides through the canopy, searching for flowers so it can eat the sweet nectar from inside.

Bromeliad

Shaped like a bucket, bromeliad plants collect rainwater. Animals in the treetops visit when they need a drink.

Coati

Coatis are climbing experts. They have curved claws, so they can move quickly and easily up and down branches.

Toucan

Toucans take short flights from tree to tree to find tasty treats. Their long bill can pluck hard-to-reach fruit out of trees.

Indri

Record-leaping indri are the largest lemurs on the island of Madagascar. They can leap 33 ft (10 m) between branches.

Tree kangaroo

With padded soles and long claws on their feet, tree kangaroos can jump easily and quickly up tree trunks to find food.

Types of forest

Forests cover 30 percent of all land on Earth. The types of forest vary depending on how far they are from the equator, an imaginary line running around the center of the Earth. Here, temperatures are hottest. The types of plants that grow in a forest also depend on the amount of rain that the forest gets.

! WOW!

Left to nature, almost **all land** on Earth would **become forest**.

Dense canopy

FACT FILE

» **Location:** South America, Southeast Asia, and West Africa

■ Rain forest

....

» **Average temperature:** Between 68 and 77°F (20 and 25°C)

....

» **Average rainfall:** 80 in+ (200 cm+)

Rain forest

Found close to the equator, rain forests only have two seasons, a wet and a dry one. Rain forest animals range from tiny frogs to huge crocodiles. One tree in the rain forest can be home to 1,000 other plants, such as vines and orchids.

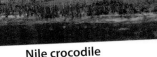

Nile crocodile

Temperate

Temperate forests have four seasons, with warm summers and cool winters. Changing temperatures mean that the animals and plants need to be ready for anything.

Maple trees

FACT FILE

» **Location:** Eastern United States, Canada, Europe, China, Japan, and parts of Russia

■ **Temperate forest**

» **Average temperature:** Between -22 and 86°F (-30 and 30°C)

» **Average rainfall:** Between 30 and 60 in (75 and 150 cm)

Brown bear catching salmon

Pine trees

Boreal

Boreal forests, also known as the taiga, grow in cold areas near the north pole. Plants and animals that live here need to be able to survive low temperatures for most of the year.

FACT FILE

» **Location:** Northern Europe, Asia, North America, and Canada

■ **Boreal forest**

» **Average temperature:** Between 23 and 41°F (-5° and 5°C)

» **Average snowfall:** Between 40 and 43 in (100 and 110 cm)

Snowshoe hare

Why are forests important?

Can you imagine what the world would be like without forests? It would be a very different place. Forests provide us with many important things such as medicines, timber, and the air that we breathe.

Soil

Forest soil is rich in nutrients because of the trees and fungi that grow in it. Soil traps water and can stop rivers from overflowing after heavy rain.

Soil holds the roots of trees.

Fungi in soil make nutrients for trees.

Jaguar

Rich wildlife

About 80 percent of the plants and animals that live on land are found in forests. Rain forests in Brazil, Madagascar, and Indonesia are home to wildlife that live nowhere else on Earth.

Sloth

Eurasian hedgehog

Books

Timber

The wood that trees are made of has many different uses. It can be used to build furniture, houses, and boats and can be turned into pulp to make paper. The book that you are reading now once started its life as a tree!

Timber

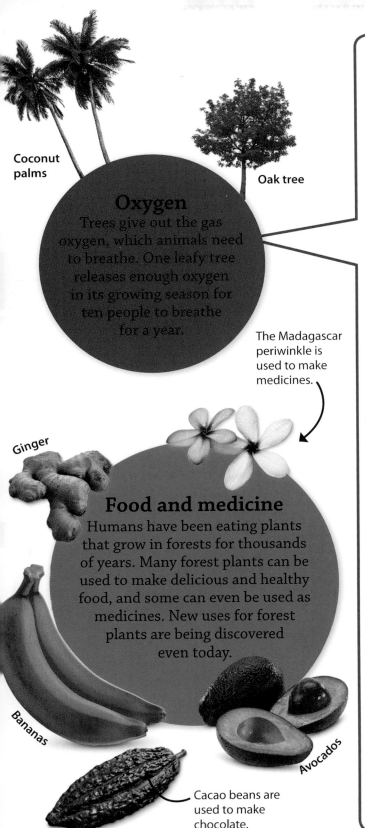

Oxygen

Trees give out the gas oxygen, which animals need to breathe. One leafy tree releases enough oxygen in its growing season for ten people to breathe for a year.

Coconut palms

Oak tree

The Madagascar periwinkle is used to make medicines.

Ginger

Food and medicine

Humans have been eating plants that grow in forests for thousands of years. Many forest plants can be used to make delicious and healthy food, and some can even be used as medicines. New uses for forest plants are being discovered even today.

Bananas

Avocados

Cacao beans are used to make chocolate.

Photosynthesis

Plants make their own food. To do this, they mix carbon dioxide from the air with water and sunlight, then release oxygen as a waste. This process is called photosynthesis.

A The roots suck up water from the ground.

B Water travels up the plant's stem.

C Carbon dioxide (CO_2) enters the leaves.

D Sunlight shines on the leaves.

E The plant uses sunlight to turn CO_2 and water into sugar for energy.

F The leaves release oxygen.

Forest communication

Under the soil in many forests around the world are secret networks of roots. The roots of plants and fungi connect and "talk" to each other and these links can be useful for many reasons. Here are some of the ways that fungi use these communication webs to protect or harm their plant neighbors.

Mushrooms

Many kinds of mushrooms grow in forests. They grow out of the ground and the part that you see on the forest floor is called the fruit. Their threadlike "roots" are always hard at work delivering secret messages underground.

Chanterelle

Beechwood sickener

Water
Some diseases cut off water to trees by damaging their roots. Fungi help fight these diseases, keeping the roots healthy and the trees alive.

Nutrients
Fungi provide trees with nutrients from the soil. In return, the trees give the fungi food, which they made using photosynthesis.

Defense
If a disease that harms trees is spreading through a forest, fungi send signals to other trees telling them to "shut down" and protect themselves.

Around **90%** of **plants** on Earth "talk" with the **fungi** that grow near them.

Beech tree
A healthy beech tree communicates with the fungi that grow around its roots.

Boletus lanatus *Amanita excelsa*

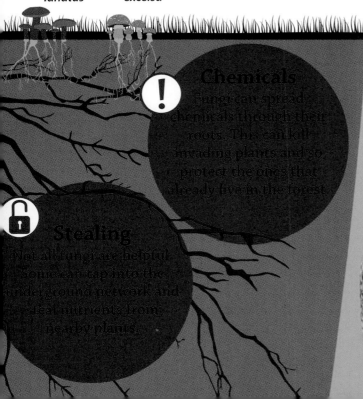

! Chemicals
Fungi can spread chemicals through their roots. This can kill invading plants and so protect the ones that already live in the forest.

🔓 Stealing
Not all fungi are helpful. Some can tap into the underground network and steal nutrients from nearby plants.

Fancy fungi

More than five million types of fungi grow in the wild. Some are small and sweet, while others can be deadly.

Death cap
You should never eat mushrooms that you find in the wild. This mushroom may look innocent, but it is very dangerous. The Ancient Greeks and Romans used it to poison their enemies.

These mushrooms look like turkeys' tails!

Turkey tail
Scientists are studying this fungus because it contains substances that may help fight colds, cancer, and infections.

Veiled lady
This fungus has a strong smell to attract insects. The insects can then carry the fungus' seedlike spores to new places so that new veiled ladies can grow.

Types of tree

Trees are not all the same. Coniferous trees keep their leaves all year round, while deciduous trees drop their leaves as it gets closer to winter. Some trees produce seeds that are transported by the wind, while other seeds are carried away by animals.

Spruce tree
These evergreen, coniferous trees can grow more than 131 ft (40 m) tall and live for hundreds of years.

FACTFILE

» **Name:** Coniferous trees

» **Examples:** Firs, Scottish pine, and redwoods

» **Location:** Boreal forests and mountains

» **Height:** Up to 380 ft (116 m)

Bunches of needles

Needles
Needles are rolled-up leaves. A waxy coating protects the needles in the winter and stops them from losing water.

Spruce cone

Cones
Seeds take a long time to grow and are protected by a cone. Young cones are green and soft, but they turn brown and hard as they reach full size.

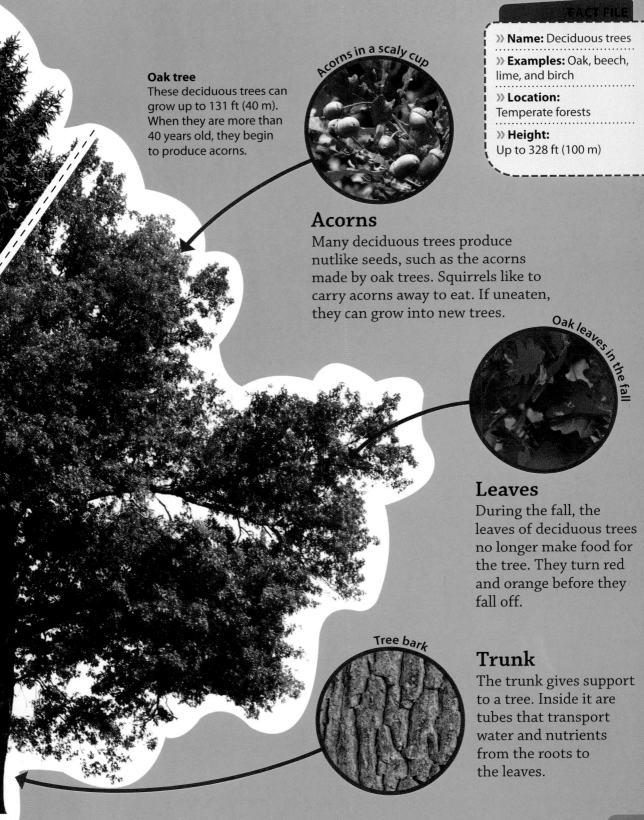

Oak tree
These deciduous trees can grow up to 131 ft (40 m). When they are more than 40 years old, they begin to produce acorns.

Acorns in a scaly cup

Acorns

Many deciduous trees produce nutlike seeds, such as the acorns made by oak trees. Squirrels like to carry acorns away to eat. If uneaten, they can grow into new trees.

Oak leaves in the fall

Leaves

During the fall, the leaves of deciduous trees no longer make food for the tree. They turn red and orange before they fall off.

Tree bark

Trunk

The trunk gives support to a tree. Inside it are tubes that transport water and nutrients from the roots to the leaves.

Mount Kinabalu

The towering Mount Kinabalu in Borneo, Southeast Asia, is 13,435 ft (4,095 m) tall. It is covered by forests from the lowlands to the mountaintop. The forests are home to a huge variety of plants and animals, and are protected in a national park.

Stinky flower

The rafflesia plant grows in Kinabalu's lowland rain forest. It has one of the world's largest flowers, which can be as wide as 40 in (100 cm). It gives off a strong smell that invites insects to feast on its pollen.

Rafflesia plant

Mountain home

Each type of forest on Mount Kinabalu has its own variety of plants and animals that have adapted to living there.

Tarsier
This small primate has large eyes so it can see at night. It can also rotate its head almost all the way around.

Pitcher plant
This beautiful plant survives by eating insects. It produces sweet-smelling nectar to lure its victims inside its flower.

Large, strong arms used to swing through the trees

Pileated gibbon
These apes live in groups and use their loud voices to stay in contact with each other when out hunting.

Yellow-breasted warbler
This small bird forages in the understory for insects and other invertebrates to eat.

Silvered leaf langur

Silvered leaf langurs live in Southeast Asia and the babies are born with bright orange fur, so they can be seen among the leaves. All the females look after the babies together in a nursery.

Darwin's frog

Darwin's frogs are found in South America, and the young are cared for by their dads. The males put the eggs inside their vocal sacs to guard them. Once the eggs turn into froglets, the male spits them out onto the forest floor.

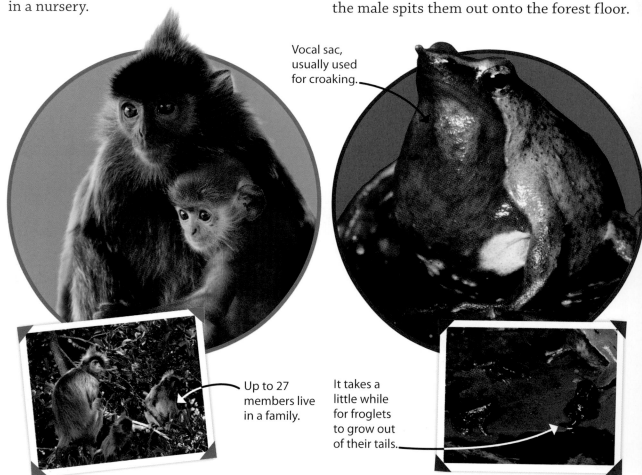

Vocal sac, usually used for croaking.

Up to 27 members live in a family.

It takes a little while for froglets to grow out of their tails.

Forest families

For some animals, bonding together in a family group helps them to survive in the forest. By working together, young can be taken care of and protected, land defended, and food found more quickly.

Collared peccary

These piglike animals live in large family groups called herds in Central and South America. They do everything as a family, including searching for food, eating, and sleeping. They bark to warn family members of danger from predators.

Termite

These social insects live in colonies all over the world. All termites have specific jobs to do, such as taking care of the eggs, raising young, building the mound, or finding food.

The queen termite is bigger than all the workers. She is the only one that lays eggs.

Peccaries snuffle around on the forest floor looking for food to eat.

Termite mounds are full of tunnels and chambers.

Family friends

Some birds flock together when forests are being cut down and finding food becomes hard. With many birds looking, they can find food more quickly and warn each other of danger.

Red-crowned ant tanager
Ants are these birds' favorite food.

Lesser woodcreeper
These birds have a large appetite for beetles and sometimes ants.

White-collared foliage gleaner
Found in Brazil, these birds like to eat bugs.

Forest birds

Birds play an important part in forest life. They can be found pecking through the leaf litter or soaring above the treetops of forests all over the world. Many birds build their nests high in the trees to keep their chicks out of reach of predators. They help the trees by feasting on tree-eating insects and scattering the trees' seeds, so that they can grow in new places in the forest.

DOWNY WOODPECKER

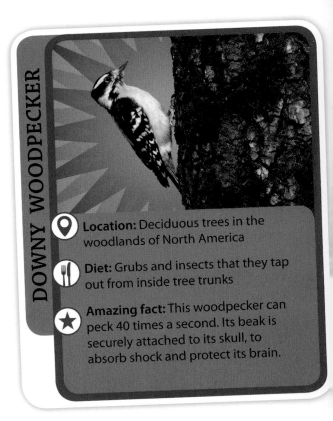

Location: Deciduous trees in the woodlands of North America

Diet: Grubs and insects that they tap out from inside tree trunks

Amazing fact: This woodpecker can peck 40 times a second. Its beak is securely attached to its skull, to absorb shock and protect its brain.

ANDEAN COCK-OF-THE-ROCK

Location: Cloud forests (also known as fog forests) of South America

Diet: Fruits, berries, and insects

Amazing fact: During mating season, the males perform dance routines to attract females. The males hop along branches and bob their heads in time with each other.

PARROT CROSSBILL

Location: Pine forests in Northern Europe, including the United Kingdom

Diet: Seeds, buds, and shoots of trees—they especially love Scottish pine

Amazing fact: Despite its name, this bird is actually a type of finch. Its beak is specially adapted to pick pine seeds out of cones.

GREAT BLUE TURACO

📍 **Location:** Rain forest canopy in African forests

🍴 **Diet:** Mainly leaves, fruit, and berries—sometimes also insects

⭐ **Amazing fact:** These birds are not very good at flying. Instead they can often be seen hopping from branch to branch in the trees.

! WOW!

Wild **peacocks** often **gather** together in **groups** called "parties."

KEEL-BILLED TOUCAN

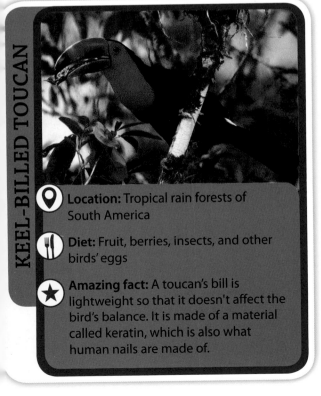

📍 **Location:** Tropical rain forests of South America

🍴 **Diet:** Fruit, berries, insects, and other birds' eggs

⭐ **Amazing fact:** A toucan's bill is lightweight so that it doesn't affect the bird's balance. It is made of a material called keratin, which is also what human nails are made of.

SNOWY OWL

📍 **Location:** Polar forest regions, including Alaska, Canada, and Siberia

🍴 **Diet:** Lemmings are their favorite, but they also eat mice, birds, and fish

⭐ **Amazing fact:** Snowy owls are the largest birds in the Arctic. They have good eyesight and sharp talons to find and snatch up prey from the snow.

Forest homes

Forests provide beds and shelter for many different animals. Some animals live in nests, high in the treetops, and others burrow deep down into the soil. All forest homes have to be safe from predators and well insulated to keep out the cold. Here are some examples of the places that animals rest their heads after a busy day, or night, in the forest.

Burrowing home

European badgers are found in the temperate forests of Europe and are master diggers. They have claws that are perfect for burrowing down into the ground. Badger burrows are called setts and are made of a series of underground tunnels and caves.

Living in the bark

Northern sportive lemurs are only found on the island of Madagascar, off the coast of Africa. They live their entire lives above ground and make their nests in the hollows of trees. These lemurs are nocturnal, which means that they sleep all day and are active at night.

Penguin parade

Snares crested penguins live on the coast of New Zealand. Every year in September, they walk up to 2,952 ft (900 m) inland to find a safe place to lay their eggs. They travel down well-worn penguin paths to reach the forests where their eggs will be safe from predators, until their young hatch a few months later.

A colony of Snares crested penguins trekking through the forest

Bed of leaves

Orangutans are found in the forests of Borneo and Sumatra, in Asia. They carefully build a new nest of leaves to sleep in every night. Youngsters learn the delicate building process from their parents, ready for when they need to make a nest of their own.

Treetop home

The American harpy eagle has a six-foot wing span and talons the size of bear claws. Each eagle can weigh up to 20 lb (9 kg), so their nests need to be very strong! They build their homes high up in the emergent layer and will use the same nest for many years.

Food chains

All living things in the forest rely on each other for food. These links can be shown in a food chain. All food chains need a producer, a consumer, and a decomposer to work well. If just one part of the food chain disappears, then it may cause many animals to go hungry!

Leaf

Producer

Food chains start with a producer, usually a green plant. Plants are producers because they make their own food from water and sunlight.

Complete the food chains

Use the clues and the descriptions below to complete the food chains.

1

Cricket
There are huge numbers of these chirping primary consumers in forests. They like to eat plants.

2

Rabbit
The teeth of these herbivores keep growing, but are worn down by all the grass they eat.

3

Maggots
These wriggling creatures look like small worms. They eat dead flesh, helping to recycle animal bodies.

4

Grass
Grass is a producer that is eaten by a huge number of herbivores all over the world.

5

Frog
Without these slippery carnivores, the world would be overrun with insects and other pests.

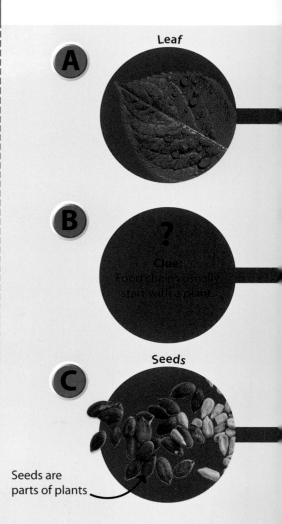

A
Leaf

B
?
Clue:
Food chains usually start with a plant.

C
Seeds

Seeds are parts of plants

Sloth

Jaguar

Dung beetle

Primary consumer

Primary consumers get their energy by eating producers. Many primary consumers are animals called herbivores, which only eat plants.

Secondary consumer

Secondary consumers get their energy by eating primary consumers. These are carnivores—predators that hunt and eat prey.

Decomposer

Decomposers break down and eat dead plants and animals. This process makes nutrients that can be absorbed by the soil.

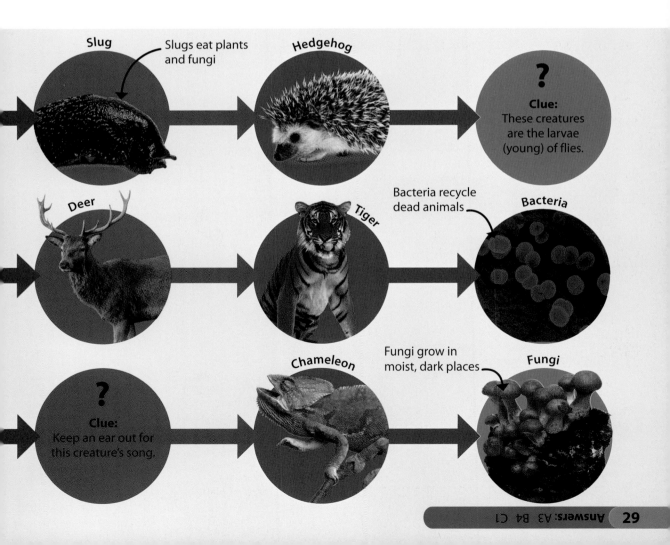

Slug — Slugs eat plants and fungi

Hedgehog

?
Clue: These creatures are the larvae (young) of flies.

Deer

Tiger

Bacteria recycle dead animals — **Bacteria**

?
Clue: Keep an ear out for this creature's song.

Chameleon

Fungi grow in moist, dark places — **Fungi**

Amazing forests

Forests grow in all shapes and sizes, and each one is special in its own way. Some have trees that are thousands of years old, and others grow under water! There is still much to learn about these amazing places.

! WOW!

Photographs taken by **satellites** have helped to find **new forests** in Africa!

Bald cypress trees in Lake Caddo, Texas

Sunken forest

Trees have been growing out of this lake for thousands of years. They have special "knees," which poke above the water's surface. Air entering the knees travels to the roots, so that the trees can survive under water.

Crooked forest

No one knows why these trees have a bend near the bottom. One theory is that people bent the trees when they were young, so that their wood could be used to build ships.

Crooked pine trees, Poland

Maquipucuna Reserve, Ecuador

Cloud forest

The canopy of this forest is cloaked in fog. It is a very hot place and this makes water vapor escape from the leaves, creating clouds. The clouds then make rain, which falls on the plants below and helps them grow.

Painted forest

The bark of these trees peels off at different times of the year. Each layer is a different color, so each peel reveals a new color. Red, green, and blue layers give a rainbow effect and make the forest look like a work of art.

Rainbow eucalyptus trees, Hawaii

Ancient Bristlecone Pine Forest, CA

Ancient forest

The oldest tree in this ancient forest is thought to be 5,066 years old—that's even older than the pyramids of Egypt. The tree's exact location is kept secret so that people don't damage it.

Living together

Many animals live in groups in the forest. Food is often spread out here, so the more animals, the larger the area they can cover to find it. Working together also means that animals can hunt larger prey. Living in a group is safer as there are more eyes to easily spot predators and animals living in families can also raise their young together.

Wolf pack

Wolves live together in packs, working as a team to hunt large prey. The group is led by an adult male and female pair.

Sharp hearing allows wolves to hear sounds from far away.

Long, powerful legs let wolves chase after prey.

Safety in numbers

Many animals live in communities in order to survive in the forest. Large groups can work together to protect themselves and their young.

Bison
Large herds of bison come together to protect their young from predators. They form circular barriers with the young sheltered in the middle.

Army ants
Army ants crawl across the forest floor in huge swarms, killing everything in their path. Their huge groups let them hunt prey bigger than themselves.

Siamangs
Siamangs are apes with very loud voices. They live in small families in Southeast Asia and make loud calls to signal if danger is nearby.

Can you see me?

Animals use camouflage to survive. Like all habitats, the forest is full of predators on the lookout for their next meal. Animals from bugs to large mammals have found ways of hiding themselves, either by blending into the background, or by looking like something that wouldn't be nice to eat.

Disguise

When the Indian leaf butterfly lands on a branch, it shows only its brown outer wings, which look exactly like a dead leaf. When it takes flight, however, it shows its true colors and flashes the bright blue of its inner wings.

Hide

Chameleons can change their color using special cells in their skin. This is often to send messages to other chameleons and show what mood they're in — for example, if they are angry. Other times, chameleons change color because of the temperature of their environment — if their skin is darker, it can absorb more heat and help them keep warm.

Illusion

Okapi live in tropical rain forests. Their rumps (backsides) have white and brown stripes, which break up the shape of their body. This makes it harder for a predator to figure out how big the okapi is, and allows it to blend into the stripy shadows of the trees.

Blend in

The fur of some animals changes throughout the year. When everything in the boreal forest is covered in snow, white fur helps the Arctic fox to disappear. When the snow melts and the ground can be seen, its fur changes to light brown.

Mimic

One good way to survive is to be a look-alike of something no one wants to eat. Giant swallowtail butterfly caterpillars look like bird poop that has dropped onto a leaf!

People in forests

Millions of people still live in tribes in forests, following a way of life that hasn't changed for thousands of years. They are skillful hunters and have an expert knowledge of which plants in the forest can treat illnesses.

An Iban tribeswoman weaves a basket from leaves.

FACT FILE

» **Name:** Iban tribe

» **Location:** Sarawak, North Borneo, Malaysia

Borneo forest

The Iban way of life is under threat, as much of their forest is being cleared for palm oil plantations. Some Iban earn money by letting tourists stay in their traditional homes, called longhouses.

Although very stinky, the durian is one of the Iban's favorite fruit.

Amazon rain forest

The Yanomami tribe has about 20,000 members, making it the largest tribe in the Amazon. The male members hunt in the forest, while the female members grow crops and prepare food.

FACT FILE

» **Name:** Yanomami tribe

» **Location:** Amazon rain forest, on the Brazil–Venezuela border

The tribe grows passion fruit to sell in local markets.

A Yanomami hunter fishes with a bow and arrow.

Himalayan forest

The Gurung live in the mountain forests of Nepal and are famous honey hunters. They hang from rope ladders and smoke out the bees so that they can collect the honey without being stung.

A honey hunter uses a stick to collect honey.

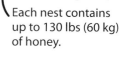

Each nest contains up to 130 lbs (60 kg) of honey.

Madagascan forest

The forest is a lifeline for the Mikea tribe of Madagascar. It provides food, water, and shelter. Each year, the tribe loses more forest as it's cut down and burned to make way for farmland.

A Mikea tribesman grates a juicy plant to get water.

In Madagascar lemurs are hunted for their meat.

Forest riches

People and animals from all over the world depend on forests. From food and wood to medicines and minerals, the forest is the world's supermarket, timber yard, pharmacy, and jewelry store rolled into one! Here are some of the useful things that come from forests.

Medicines
Medicines for lots of illnesses come from plants. Scientists explore forests to search for plants containing natural chemicals that can be used to make people well.

Chamomile
Mixed with hot water, these daisylike flowers make a soothing tea that can help treat many illnesses.

Elderberry
The flowers and berries of this small tree are used to make many drinks that are good for the human body.

Wild garlic
The leaves of this forest-floor plant can help to reduce blood pressure.

Cranberries
These red berries are the fruit of low-lying vines. They are packed full of nutrients, some of which can fight infections.

Wooden basket
Wood can be used to make useful items, such as baskets, barrels, and other containers.

Wood
People have been using wood from forests for thousands of years to build houses, make furniture, and use as a fuel.

Minerals

Minerals such as precious metals and stones are found under rain forests in many parts of the world. Mining, or digging for, minerals means that large areas of ancient rain forest are cut down.

Topaz

Ruby

Gold

Emerald

Diamond

Pineapple
This juicy fruit grows in the rain forest understory.

Grapes
Bunches of wild grapes grow in forest canopies all over the world and provide a feast for birds.

Bananas
There are over 50 types of bananas that grow in tropical forests. Other types are also grown in over 150 countries for humans to eat.

Food

A lot of the foods that we eat today grow wild in forests. Farmers also grow these foods in large amounts in fields and orchards to supply our supermarkets.

Tomatoes
Really a fruit and not a vegetable, the tomato originally came from South America.

Mushrooms
Some forest-floor mushrooms are delicious, but others are deadly.

Cacao beans
All chocolate starts its life in a rain forest as a cacao bean.

Forest seasons

In temperate parts of the world, there are four seasons in a year. The forests in these regions look very different during each season because the trees shed their leaves in preparation for winter. Forest animals find winters difficult, and many move away or hibernate to survive the cold months.

Fall

Colorful leaves

In fall the leaves of many trees begin to change to red, orange, and gold, as they die and fall off. As the days become shorter and colder, animals prepare their dens while others take off for warmer lands.

Lush leaves

Plants continue to grow, and the leaves of the canopy shade the forest floor. Many plants produce fruit, so there is plenty of food for animals and their young.

Summer

REALLY?

Tropical rain forests have just **two** seasons: a **rainy** season and a **dry** season.

Hibernation

Many animals, including hedgehogs, spend winter in a sleeplike state called hibernation. They hide among tree roots, piles of rocks, or fallen leaves and stay there until spring.

Hibernating hedgehog

Winter

Spring

Falling snow

Many of the trees have lost their leaves and their branches are bare. The weather is cold, and there may be frost and snow. Animals have to search hard to find food.

Blooming flowers

Forest-floor flowers, such as bluebells, burst through the soil, capturing the sunlight before the trees grow leaves and block it out. Animals begin to search for food after winter, and have young as the weather becomes warmer.

Insects

There are thousands of different types of insect living in forests, and they all play an important role. Insects help many trees and other forest plants make seeds, which can grow into new plants. They also eat dead trees, releasing the nutrients from the wood back into the soil.

A sparrow snacks on an ant.

Eat or be eaten

Insects are important to the survival of the forest and the animals that live there. They form parts of many food chains. Lots of insects are prey that are eaten by other animals. But some insects are predators and excellent hunters. The praying mantis, for example, is an expert at catching other insects and spiders.

Helping plants make seeds

Bees and other insects help plants make seeds. They do this by picking up pollen grains when they come to feed on nectar, which is a sweet liquid made by flowers. The insects then spread the pollen to other flowers, which use it to make seeds.

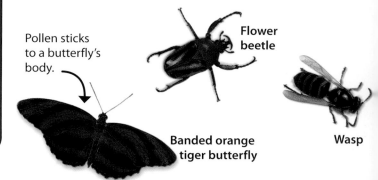

Pollen sticks to a butterfly's body.

Flower beetle

Banded orange tiger butterfly

Wasp

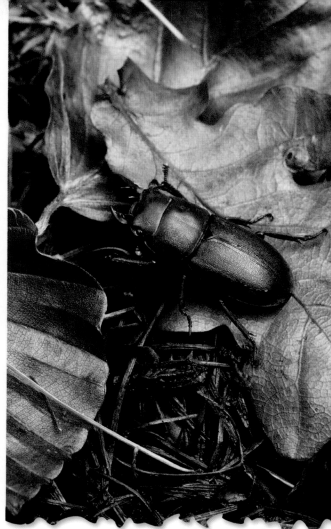

Feeding on dead trees

When a tree dies, many insects use it as food. Bark beetles drill holes into the tree and lay eggs there. Their young then eat the bark and wood. The holes let other insects get inside the tree and feed there, too. Fungi also live off dead wood.

Reusing nutrients

When an insect, such as a stag beetle, eats some wood, it breaks it down in its gut. Some of the nutrients from the wood help the insect grow, but other nutrients are passed out of the insect's body in its waste. This becomes part of the soil that plants can use.

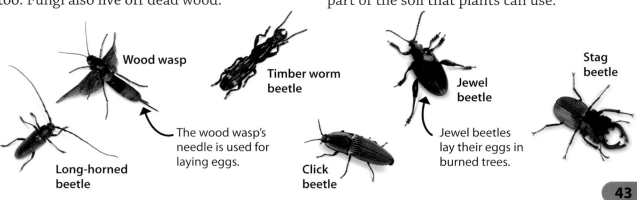

Wood wasp

Timber worm beetle

Jewel beetle

Stag beetle

The wood wasp's needle is used for laying eggs.

Long-horned beetle

Click beetle

Jewel beetles lay their eggs in burned trees.

Migration

Forest plants and animals have found many ways to survive. Some animals take long journeys, called migrations, moving from place to place. They move in search of water, food, and warmth, and return to the best places to give birth to their young. Many of these animal migrations happen over a year. The forests themselves can also migrate, although this takes many thousands of years.

Help to migrate

Some forests need help to survive because of changing habitats and humans cutting down trees. People can help by collecting and replanting saplings in other places where they can grow well.

Planting saplings

Forest

Over thousands of years, Earth's climate has changed, and different types of forest have grown in new places. For example, the climate has become warmer, so trees that prefer cold places have been found growing farther north.

Woodland caribou

Woodland caribou are found in North America, Russia, and Northern Europe. Every summer they travel more than 600 miles (966 km) to different forests to feed on new grasses.

Umbrella bird

These tropical rain forest birds, found in South America, migrate into the high mountains to mate. They then return to the lower areas of the rain forest to lay their eggs.

Monarch butterfly

Monarch butterflies living in the eastern states of the US migrate more than 2,500 miles (4,000 km) south to Mexico. Here, they eat and stay warm over winter, then return north to lay their eggs.

Blowing in the wind
The seeds of many trees are specially shaped so that they can be blown over long distances in the wind. If the conditions are right for growing where they land, new forests appear.

Running fast
Caribou can run as fast as 50 mph (80 kph) when on the move or escaping from predators such as wolves.

Impressive hair
Male umbrella birds show off with displays to attract females. They raise their head crests, and also enlarge their necks, or wattles, to make a loud booming sound.

Finding the right trees
Monarch butterflies migrate to the same oyamel fir trees in Mexico's forests every year. Different butterflies make the journey for the first time each year. However, they always know exactly where to go.

Sounds of the forest

Trumpet, buzz, screech, shout, scream, bellow! The forest can be a very loud place. Animals cannot always see or find each other through the dense trees. That's why they make all these sounds—to "talk," or communicate, with each other.

Singing cicada

These bugs are found all over the world and use a part of their body, called a tymbal, to "sing." Only the male cicadas sing, to attract female mates.

Each species of cicada has its own song.

Bellowing stag

Red deer live in Europe, Asia, and North America. The males, called stags, are known for bellowing loudly during the breeding season. The stags use these sounds to attract female deer, called hinds, and to scare away rival stags.

Purring lemur

Ring-tailed lemurs purr to the other members of their group. This soothing sound helps them form close bonds. They are only found in Madagascar and have more than 30 different calls, each one signaling a different message.

Alarm calls are important for staying safe.

Howling monkey

Howler monkeys, found in Central and South America, howl in groups, called troops, every morning. They do this to tell others that this part of the forest belongs to them. They usually choose areas that contain lots of their favorite fruit.

The clicks tell predators: "I'm not tasty!"

Clicking moth

Moths such as tiger moths can give off little high-pitched clicks to "talk" to each other and to scare away predators such as bats. These moths live in Europe, Asia, and North America, and some of them can click 4,500 times a second!

Roaring gorilla

The safest way for the African silverback gorilla to guard his troop is to be extremely loud and look very threatening. A silverback will roar, pull branches, and jump around to defend his territory.

Elephant rumble

Using low rumbles, Asian forest elephants can communicate with each other over several miles. These noises are so low-pitched that humans can't always hear them.

This gorilla shows his teeth as a threat.

Walk through the forest

Forests are exciting places, but it can be very easy to lose your way in them. These helpful hints will show you how to navigate your way through a forest. Always make sure you stick to the forest code!

Look for a river or stream.

Follow the water

Towns, villages, and campsites are usually built next to a river. By following a stream or river downstream, you are likely to come across a settlement.

Find south.

Use the Sun

As well as a compass, you can use a watch and the Sun to find south. Point your watch's hour hand at the Sun. The halfway point between the hour hand and 12 is south.

Find north.

Look at the lichen

Lichen and moss can help you get your bearings, too. They usually grow better on the north-facing side of trees, as they like shade.

Use a shadow

Put a stick in the ground, and mark the end of its shadow. Mark the end of the shadow again after 15 minutes. The line between these two marks runs from west to east.

Look for a road.

Find west and east.

Climb a tree

With great care, climb up a tree and look at the surrounding forest. A dip in the tops of the trees means that there is a road, river, or clearing there.

Mark your trail

Leave small mounds of stones or twigs along your path. These markers can help you retrace your steps if you pass them when lost.

Leave markers.

Look to the sky.

Use the stars

If it is night, you can use the stars to guide you. In northern parts of the Earth, the North Star points north. In southern parts of the Earth, the Southern Cross can direct you south.

Forest code

Always go with a group. ✓

Tell someone where you're going and when you're going to be back. ✓

Bring a compass. ✓

Bring a phone (fully charged). ✓

Take more food and water than you think you'll need. ✓

Bring a map. ✓

Wear comfortable shoes and clothes. ✓

Grand Teton National Park

Since opening in 1929, millions of people have visited Grand Teton National Park in Wyoming. The park is one of the largest temperate forests in the world, and visitors are treated to a forest landscape that has remained the same since prehistoric times.

Park ranger with visitors

Park rangers
A park ranger's job includes protecting the wildlife and managing forest fires. They also guide visitors around the park and keep them safe.

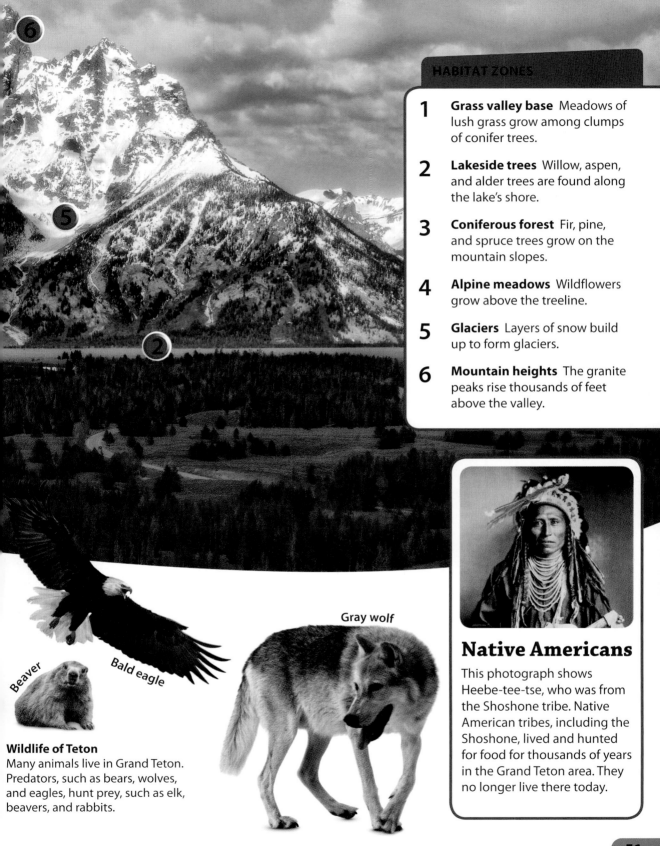

6

5

2

HABITAT ZONES

1 **Grass valley base** Meadows of lush grass grow among clumps of conifer trees.

2 **Lakeside trees** Willow, aspen, and alder trees are found along the lake's shore.

3 **Coniferous forest** Fir, pine, and spruce trees grow on the mountain slopes.

4 **Alpine meadows** Wildflowers grow above the treeline.

5 **Glaciers** Layers of snow build up to form glaciers.

6 **Mountain heights** The granite peaks rise thousands of feet above the valley.

Gray wolf

Beaver

Bald eagle

Wildlife of Teton
Many animals live in Grand Teton. Predators, such as bears, wolves, and eagles, hunt prey, such as elk, beavers, and rabbits.

Native Americans
This photograph shows Heebe-tee-tse, who was from the Shoshone tribe. Native American tribes, including the Shoshone, lived and hunted for food for thousands of years in the Grand Teton area. They no longer live there today.

51

Forest fires

Forest fires are a natural way for a forest to renew and regrow. A forest fire can start naturally anywhere in the world when lightning strikes trees or plants. These are called wildfires. Here are some of the good things that forest fires can do for forests.

WOW!

Forest rangers in the US sometimes start fires to **control** the **size** of **forests.**

Soil
After a fire, the forest is covered in a layer of ash. This ash mixes into the soil, making it rich in nutrients for new plants to grow.

Seeds
Jack pine seeds start to grow in the heat of a forest fire. Once the fire is finished, new shoots burst through the ground.

Dead wood
Dead burned wood has cracks, which provide ideal shelter for many small animals, such as mice, reptiles, and birds.

Fiery feast

Once a forest fire has died away, many animals come to the area to find food.

Bark beetle This burrowing beetle feeds on the burned wood.

Black-backed woodpecker This bird feasts on the insects.

Vulture This bird scavenges on any animals that didn't survive the fire.

New trees

Over time, grasses, shrubs, and then small trees grow on the forest floor. Eventually, the new plants will cover the burned ground.

Forest

Some forests take hundreds of years to fully regrow after a fire. Pine forests recover more quickly and can regrow completely in 40 years.

Deforestation and conservation

Forests are important to us and the health of the planet. However, large areas of forest are cut down every year to make space for farmland and housing—this is called deforestation. Forests need to be protected and there are many ways that we can all help.

Fields for animals

As large herds of cows are needed for food, forests are cut down to make space for them to graze. If less meat was eaten, fewer herds would be needed and forests would be safer.

Cattle

Tree products

Many trees are cut down to make wooden furniture and paper used by people all over the world.

Wooden cabinet

Palm oil

Mangroves and rain forests are cut down to make space for oil palm tree plantations. Palm oil is used in many things such as shampoo, soap, and chocolate.

Oil palm fruits

Deforestation

Useful plants

Some plants produce oils that can keep us healthy. By learning more about plants and what they can do for humans, their habitats can be protected.

Aloe vera

Eucalyptus

New Forest National Park, UK

Conservation sites

National parks are protected areas for animals and plants. Within these parks, people cannot cut down trees or let animals graze.

Oak tree beginning to grow

Reforestation

The Forest Stewardship Council (FSC) works with companies to take care of forests. For every tree that is cut down, another is planted.

Conservation

Recycle

By recycling paper and other products made from wood, companies can avoid cutting down more trees. Old cards, wrapping paper, and magazines can be recycled to make new ones.

Meet the expert

We put some questions to Alexis Hatto, whose job it is to protect forests and the animals that live there. Much of his work involves advising palm oil companies on how to avoid clearing forests and how they can help protect wildlife.

Q: We know it is something to do with forests, but what is your actual job?

A: I work for the Zoological Society of London, which is a wildlife conservation charity that helps protect animals and their habitats. My job involves working with companies all over the world to help them reduce the bad effects that they might have on the natural world. I help these companies reduce pollution and protect important habitats like forests.

Q: Why are forests important?

A: Forests are really important because they contain a lot of biodiversity, which means there are lots of plants and animals living in them. Tropical forests do really important jobs, such as keeping our climate steady and cleaning the air we breathe. When pollution happens or trees are cut down without being replaced, forests struggle to do these jobs.

Oil palm plantation
Forest is cleared for palms, which are grown for their oil.

Oil palm fruit

This can have a harmful knock-on effect for the plants and animals that live there, and also for people all over the world.

Q: What made you decide to work in forests?

A: I am a "tree hugger" and I love forests! Sadly, I couldn't find a job that would pay me to hug trees. I wanted a job that would allow me to protect forests and to spend time in them. I care a lot about all the animals and plants that live there, and this job helps protect them. I wanted to do a job where I could help people realize how important forests are.

Q: What is a typical work day for you?

A: My team works directly with palm oil companies to make sure they have made responsible plans to manage their land and the water in the area. This then helps our scientists in Indonesia and Thailand protect endangered animals such as tigers and elephants. Palm oil is an oil that comes from the fruit of the oil palm tree. It is used in many different everyday things such as some types of shampoo, ice cream, and cleaning products.

Q: What do you love most about the forests that you work in?

A: I love all the noises that animals make in the forest. My favorite forest animals are the primates, including orangutans and siamangs, but also the monkeys, lorises, and tarsiers. They remind me of how closely we are related to other animals. It feels very special for me to see these animals in the wild and know that my job protects them.

Slender loris

Q: What is the most difficult part of your job?

A: My job is all about trying to get people and companies to act sustainably, which can be difficult. It means making sure the way we live today doesn't harm the world, so that animals, including humans, can live here in the future. Trying to convince people to act in a certain way is hard, as they might not understand the effects of their actions.

Q: What is the best thing about your job?

A: I really enjoy inspiring people to take action and protect the natural world. I love that the work I do helps forest plants and animals survive. I really enjoy helping people understand where their food comes from, so that they can choose things that are more sustainable. Every day brings new challenges, and I am really lucky that I get to visit the amazing forests that I help protect.

Forest facts and figures

The world's forests are incredible places that are full of life. Here are some amazing forest facts that you might not have heard before.

Chestnut-eared aracari

33%
of the **world's bird species** live in the **Amazon rain forest**.

More than **20%** of the world's **oxygen** is produced in the **Amazon rain forest**.

Most **forest trees** need to be exposed to **fire** every **50–100 years** to help them **grow**.

50
So many trees are cut down every day that it is the same as losing about 50 soccer fields of forest every minute.

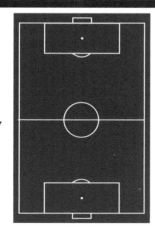

25%
More than 25% of all medicines used today come from the rain forest.

The Amazon camu camu berry is full of vitamin.

One large tree can provide **a day's supply of oxygen** for **up to four people.**

If you find a **tree stump**, you can figure out how old it is by **counting** the **rings** in the wood.

Forests cover about 30% of the land on Earth.

A **falling raindrop** can take **10 minutes** to travel from the **treetop canopy** to the **forest floor.**

The **tallest tree** in the world is a **Redwood** named **Hyperion**. It measures **379 ft 8 in (115.7 m)**. This is the same height as **20** two-story **houses** stacked on top of each other.

100

It is estimated that in 100 years' time, there will be no rain forests left.

280

One oak tree can support over 280 species of insects.

Speckled wood butterfly

2.2

tons (2 metric tons) of timber make just 1.1 tons (1 metric ton) of paper.

Glossary

Here are the meanings of some words that are useful for you to know when learning about forests.

adapted When an animal or plant becomes better suited to its habitat. For example, a penguin's thick feathers keep it warm in icy places

bacteria Tiny living things that can be found everywhere on Earth, such as inside food, soil, or even the human body

biodiversity Variety of plants and animals that live in an area

bonding When families become emotionally attached to one another

camouflage Colors or patterns on an animal's skin, fur, or feathers that help it blend in with the environment

carnivore Animal that eats only meat

climate Area that has particular weather conditions

conifer Type of tree with cones and needlelike leaves

conservation Trying to stop an animal or plant from becoming extinct

consumer Animal that eats plants or other animals

crops Group of plants that are grown as food

deciduous tree Tree that loses its leaves in winter

decomposer Living thing, often a fungus, that breaks down dead matter to create nutrients

deforestation Destruction of forests

endangered When an animal or plant species is in danger of dying out

environment Place where an animal or plant lives

equator Imaginary line around the center of the Earth that is equal distance from the north and south poles

fossil Remains of a dead animal or plant, which has been preserved in rock over time

fuel Substance that is burned for heat or power

fungi Living things such as mushrooms and molds that break down dead plants and animals to make their food

habitat Place where a plant or animal lives

herbivore Animal that eats only plant matter

herd Group of animals

insulated When something is covered in a material that does not allow heat to pass easily through it

invertebrate Animal that does not have a backbone

lichen Type of fungus that lives in a partnership with an alga or bacterium

lowland Land that is no higher than 660 ft (200 m) above sea level

migration Regular movement of animals, often to feed or breed

mimic Animal that copies the appearance or behavior of another

nectar Sweet liquid made by some flowers

nocturnal When animals sleep during the day and are active at night

nursery Place where young animals or plants are taken care of together

nutrients Types of food that animals need to survive

photosynthesis Process that green plants use to make food

plantation Place where crops are grown

predator Animal that hunts other living animals for food

pollution Harmful substances in the air, soil, or water

prehistoric Something that happened or was around in ancient times before recorded history

prey Animal that is hunted for food

primate Group of mammals that includes monkeys

producer Living thing such as a plant that makes its own food and is eaten by animals

recycle Use something old to make something new

reforestation When forests regrow naturally or are planted by humans

satellites Machines that are placed above the Earth to monitor conditions on Earth and send messages

scavenger Animal that feeds on the leftover meat of another animal that has already died, whether by a predator attack or natural causes

species Specific types of animals or plants with shared features that can produce young together

sustainable Able to be supported for a long time

temperate When an area or climate has mild temperatures

territory Area that is owned by a certain group of animals or people

traditional When something has been done in the same way for a long time

tropical When an area or climate has hot temperatures and high rainfall

vegetation Plant life found in a particular habitat

water vapor Gas that is made when water is heated

Index

Acknowledgments

DORLING KINDERSLEY would like to thank: Jolyon Goddard, Deborah Lock, Satu Fox, Manisha Majithia, and Megan Weal for editorial assistance, Bettina Myklebust Stovne and Jaileen Kaur for design assistance, Suresh Kumar for cartography, Molly Lattin and Dan Crisp for illustrations, Jacqueline Harris for educational consulting, Caroline Hunt for proofreading, and Hilary Bird for the index. The publishers would also like to thank Alexis Hatto for the "Meet the expert" interview.

The publisher would like to thank the following for their kind permission to reproduce their photographs:

(Key: a-above; b-below/bottom; c-center; f-far; l-left; r-right; t-top)

2 123RF.com: Tomas Hajek (bl). Dorling Kindersley: Jerry Young (bc). 3 Alamy Stock Photo: Niels Poulsen (bl). Dorling Kindersley: Blackpool Zoo, Lancashire, UK (bc); Natural History Museum, London (tr); British Wildlife Centre, Surrey, UK (br). 4 Getty Images: Martin Harvey / Photodisc (ca). 4-5 Alamy Stock Photo: Helen Dixon (c). 6 Alamy Stock Photo: hannah russell (crb); Kevin Schafer (tl). 7 Alamy Stock Photo: David Noton Photography (br); Edward Parker (clb). 10 123RF.com: Panu Ruangjan / panuruangjan (br). Alamy Stock Photo: Zena Elea (clb); blickwinkel / Meyers (cla). 11 Alamy Stock Photo: Nick Garbutt / Steve Bloom Images (br); Lívio Soares de Medeiros (cra). naturepl.com: Roland Seitre (bl). 12 Alamy Stock Photo: Dave Marsden (br); Kevin Schafer (tl). 13 Alamy Stock Photo: Thomas Kitchin & Victoria Hurst / Design Pics Inc (bl); Sean Pavone (ca); JTB Photo \ UIG (cr); Grigory Pil (bc). 14 123RF.com: Visarute Angkatavanich (cl); vilainecrevette (cb); Mariya Ermolaeva (ca). Dorling Kindersley: Jerry Young (clb). iStockphoto.com: Vitalina (br). 15 123RF.com: Tomas Hajek (bl); pretoperola (tl); zerbor (tc). Alamy Stock Photo: Nirmal Kulkarni / ephotocorp (c). 17 Alamy Stock Photo: Gabbro (br); Niels Poulsen (cra); Wild Life Ranger (cr). 18 Alamy Stock Photo: blickwinkel / Hecker (r). 19 Alamy Stock Photo: Arndt Sven-Erik / Arterra Picture Library (bc). Getty Images: DNY59 (l). 20 Alamy Stock Photo: Nokuro (bl). 20-21 Getty Images: John W Banagan. 21 Alamy Stock Photo: FLPA (br); Ingmar Zahorsky (ca); Svetlana Foote (cb). Dorling Kindersley: Thomas Marent (cr). 22 Alamy Stock Photo: Louise Heusinkveld (clb); Christian Kober / robertharding (cla); Michael & Patricia Fogden / Minden Pictures (cr); Michael & Patricia Fogden / Minden Pictures (crb). 23 Alamy Stock Photo: Larry Ditto / DanitaDelimont.com (cl); Ray Wilson (cb). Dreamstime.com: Nenotarsatika (crb); Werayut Nueathong (cr). Getty Images: Glenn Bartley

(crb/Woodcreeper); Danita Delimont (clb). WorldWildlifeImages.com / Andy & Gill Swash: (fcrb). 24 Alamy Stock Photo: Tom and Pam Gardner / FLPA / imageBROKER (clb); Male Downy Woodpecker (tr); Kit Day (crb). 25 Alamy Stock Photo: Phil Crosby (tl). Dorling Kindersley. Getty Images: Sandy Carey, Photodisc / Alan (crb). 26 Alamy Stock Photo: Marko König / imageBROKER (bl); Thomas Marent / Rolfnp (br). 27 Alamy Stock Photo: blickwinkel / Hummel (br); Frans Lanting (tr); Arco Images / Wegner, P. (bl). 28 Getty Images: DAJ (cr). 29 Dorling Kindersley: British Wildlife Centre, Surrey, UK (clb). Fotolia: Eric Isselee (tc). Science Photo Library: Dr Kari Lounatmaa (crb). 30 Alamy Stock Photo: Maciej Bledowski (br). Dreamstime.com: Maxim Petrichuk (cl). 31 Alamy Stock Photo: Dennis Frates (cr); Maximilian Weinzierl (tl). 32-33 Alamy Stock Photo: Michael Weber / imageBROKER. 33 Alamy Stock Photo: Gabriela Insuratelu (br); Premaphotos (cra). naturepl.com: Delpho / ARCO (cra). 34 123RF.com: Oxana Brigadirova / Iarus (b). Dorling Kindersley. 35 Alamy Stock Photo: Guenter Fischer / imageBROKER (bl); i animal (tl); Jamen Percy (br). 36 iStockphoto.com: luoman (br); robas (cla). 37 Alamy Stock Photo: Frans Lanting Studio (clb). Dima Chatrov: (cra). 39 Dorling Kindersley: Natural History Museum (tr); Natural History Museum (cra). Dreamstime.com: Broodwolf (c). 40 Alamy Stock Photo: PaulPaladin (br); Jochen Schlenker / robertharding (tr). 41 Alamy Stock Photo: Anna Stowe Landscapes UK (bl); Helen Dixon (tl); Frank Hecker (cra). 42 123RF.com: pedarilhos (tr); Ryszard Stelmachowicz (clb). 43 Alamy Stock Photo: Jason Bazzano (fclb); Paul R. Sterry / Nature Photographers Ltd (clb); Scott Camazine (cb). iStockphoto.com: Henrik_L (tl); merlinpf (tr). 44-45 Alamy Stock Photo: blickwinkel (bl); Mint Images Limited (ca); Don Johnston_IH (b). Getty Images: Nacivet / Photographer's Choice (cb). 44 Alamy Stock Photo: AndreyPopov / Panther Media GmbH (bl). 45 Alamy Stock Photo: Naturepix (crb). 46 Alamy Stock Photo: G. Aunion Juan (br); Patrick Lynch (cra); Michael Krabs / imageBROKER (tr). 47 Alamy Stock Photo: Andrey Gudkov / Steve Bloom Images (br); Octavio Campos Salles (tl). Dorling

Kindersley: Natural History Museum, London (ca). 49 Dreamstime.com: Teemu Tretjakov (clb). Getty Images: Noll Images (c). 50-51 Getty Images: Jeff R Clow. 50 Alamy Stock Photo: Jim West (crb). 51 Alamy Stock Photo: The Protected Art Archive (crb); herbertschroer / RooM the Agency (bl). Dorling Kindersley: Jerry Young (bc). 52-53 Getty Images: Pascal Parrot / Sygma. 53 Alamy Stock Photo: Glenn Bartley / All Canada Photos (cr). Ardea: Nigel Cattlin / Science Source (cra). 54 Alamy Stock Photo: dolphfyn (bc). Getty Images: Photo by Cody Cobb (r). 55 Getty Images: Adam Burton / robertharding (l); Oscar Wong / Moment Open (tr). 56 Zoological Society of London: Alexis Hatto (ar). Dreamstime.com: Ahmad Fairuzazli (crb). FLPA: Thomas Marent (b). 57 Alamy Stock Photo: UNTAMED / Hornbill Images (tr). 58 Alamy Stock Photo: Ildi.Food (br). Dorling Kindersley. 59 Alamy Stock Photo: Mint Images - Frans Lanting (bl). Dorling Kindersley: Natural History Museum, London (bc). 60 Dorling Kindersley: Jerry Young (bl).

Cover images: Front: 123RF.com: Tomas Hajek cb; Alamy Stock Photo: Michael Krabs / imageBROKER l, Lívio Soares de Medeiros tr; Dorling Kindersley: Blackpool Zoo, Lancashire, UK bc, Jerry Young cra; Back: Alamy Stock Photo: Svetlana Foote tr; Dorling Kindersley: Thomas Marent cr; Front Flap: 123RF.com: Visarute Angkatavanich cr, Panu Ruangjan / panuruangjan cla; Alamy Stock Photo: FLPA br, Male Downy Woodpecker cra; iStockphoto.com: Vitalina cl; Back Flap: Dorling Kindersley: Natural History Museum, London cb; iStockphoto.com: Naumoid tr; Front Endpapers: Alamy Stock Photo: Nigel Hicks 0br; Dorling Kindersley: Batsford Garden Centre and Arboretum 0bc

All other images © Dorling Kindersley
For further information see: www.dkimages.com

My Findout facts:

Heights of trees

Ancient trees

Some trees have been on Earth for thousands of years. Fossilized, or preserved, parts of ginkgo trees have been found that date back 190 million years. Some tree fern fossils are even older—dating back 250 million years!

Tree ferns

Ginkgo

305 ft
(93 m)

English oak makes very hard and sturdy timber.

132 ft
(40 m)

81.5 ft
(25 m)

The umbrella tree's flowers smell horrible!

36 ft
(11 m)

The trunk can store 26,400 gallons (100,000 liters) of water.

Statue of Liberty, New York City
This famous American monument weighs 225 tons (204 metric tons).

Umbrella tree, North America
This small tree has clusters of large umbrella-like leaves.

Baobab, Senegal, Africa
The thick trunk of a baobab can measure up to 154 ft (47 m) all the way around.

English oak, UK, Europe
This tree does not produce acorns, or oak nuts, until it's at least 40 years old.